W9-BPL-090

BASKETBALL'S
NEW
WAVE

THE YOUNG SUPERSTARS
TAKING OVER THE GAME

BRIAN MAHONEY

First Edition
Second Printing, 2019

Book design by Sarah Taplin
Cover design by Sarah Taplin
Photographs ©: Aaron Gash/AP Images, cover (center), 1 (center); Matt Slocum/AP Images, cover (left), 1 (left), 61, 92–93; Jim Mone/AP Images, cover (right), 1 (right), 8–9, back cover; Craig Mitchelldyer/AP Images, 4; Nick Wass/AP Images, 12, 52–53, 88; LM Otero/AP Images, 15; Rick Scuteri/AP Images, 20; Rick Bowmer/AP Images, 24–25, 80, 84–85; Elise Amendola/AP Images, 28, 98–99; David J. Phillip/AP Images, 34; John Amis/AP Images, 39, 112; Gerald Herbert/AP Images, 42; Tyler Kaufman/AP Images, 46–47; Tony Gutierrez/AP Images, 50, 72; Chris Szagola/AP Images, 58; Mark Blinch/The Canadian Press/AP Images, 66; Julie Jacobson/AP Images, 70; Mark J. Terrill/AP Images, 76–77; Darren Abate/AP Images, 96; Bruce Kluckhohn/AP Images, 104; Andy Clayton-King/AP Images, 109; Marcio Jose Sanchez/AP Images, 117

Design Elements ©: Shutterstock

Press Box Books, an imprint of Press Room Editions.

Library of Congress Control Number: 2019937098

ISBN
978-1-63494-087-0 (paperback)
978-1-63494-088-7 (epub)
978-1-63494-089-4 (hosted ebook)

Distributed by North Star Editions, Inc.
2297 Waters Drive
Mendota Heights, MN 55120
www.northstareditions.com
Printed in the United States of America

TABLE OF CONTENTS

CHAPTER 1

STEVEN ADAMS

As the youngest of 18 children in his family, Steven Adams had to learn to stick up for himself. If not, his older siblings could make things hard on him. His brothers average 6 feet 9 inches, and even his sisters average 6 feet. So, from an early age, Adams had to figure out how to hold his own against big, strong competition.

"They do teach me a lot of things," Adams said. "I was more competitive because I was always the weakest. . . . Playing against my sisters and my brothers, the older ones would play really rough and elbow you. Plus, the younger ones did a little, too."

No wonder he became one of the toughest players in the National Basketball Association (NBA).

Even in the NBA, Steven Adams often towers over the opposition.

Battling against opponents his own size is no big deal for Adams. While his Oklahoma City Thunder have had great scorers such as Kevin Durant, Russell Westbrook, and Paul George over the years, Adams has never been one to worry about his points. The burly center instead takes on the tough tasks such as setting screens so his teammates can get open and being a rugged rebounder and defender.

ADAMS AND HIS SUPERSTAR BIG SISTER

Even with all his NBA success, Adams isn't even the most accomplished athlete in his family. His half-sister Valerie was the Olympic gold medalist in the shot put in 2008 and 2012. She also won the silver medal in 2016 and remains one of the best in the world. Representing New Zealand, she was unbeaten in major world events from 2006 through 2014. Competing with her when he was younger and watching her train as an adult helped teach Steven lessons he would need to be successful in his own career.

"I thought I worked hard, and a lot of people say I do, as well, but seeing her work is on a whole other level. It's absolutely unbelievable. (She's) the most disciplined person in the world and just the hardest worker," he said.

"He can have a huge impact on our team," Thunder general manager Sam Presti said before the 2018–19 season. "And the reason he's so valuable to us, he has such a big impact on our team by doing the things that are within his control."

Growing up, Adams played rugby, the most popular sport in his home country of New Zealand. But with his size and skills, it soon became clear that his future would be in basketball.

An imposing presence, Adams is 7 feet tall and 265 pounds, with long hair and a thick beard. He possesses strength that is common among rugby players but sets him apart against most of his rivals on the basketball court.

> **"THAT GUY IS THE STRONGEST, MOST PHYSICAL GUY IN THE LEAGUE."**
>
> **–FORMER THUNDER COACH SCOTT BROOKS**

"That guy is the strongest, most physical guy in the league," said Scott Brooks, Adams's former coach in Oklahoma City.

But Adams isn't only just about force. He also can show finesse, with a nice shooting touch. During the 2017–18 season, he finished fourth in the NBA in field-goal percentage, making 63 percent of his shots.

Adams uses has massive size and strength to dominate under the basket for the Thunder.

He even had one night when he couldn't miss from anywhere. He made all 11 shots from the field and was a perfect on his five free-throw attempts.

Adams also tied for the NBA lead that season by averaging 5.1 offensive rebounds per game. He not only

is powerful enough to get good rebounding position; he's also adept at gauging how the ball is going to bounce off the rim so he can quickly pursue it.

Once he started to show those talents as a teenager, he became a promising prospect. Jamie Dixon, who was the coach at the University of Pittsburgh, had played professionally and later coached in New Zealand. He persuaded Adams to come play for him. After one season in college, Adams was taken by the Thunder with the No. 12 pick in the 2013 draft. That made him the first player from New Zealand to be a first-round pick in the NBA Draft.

Unlike most players drafted that high, Adams wasn't going to a struggling or rebuilding team. The Thunder, already one of the best teams in the league, had traded for the pick. Oklahoma City needed Adams to be productive right away. In Adams's first season, the Thunder went all the way to the Western Conference Finals. They got back there again in his third season, falling just one win short of making the NBA Finals.

Adams would continue to increase his scoring average as the years went on, but he rarely made it a priority unless the Thunder needed it.

"He just wants to win, and that's all that matters to him," Westbrook said.

That didn't always make Adams popular with his opponents. The *Los Angeles Times* polled players in 2016, and they voted Adams the second-dirtiest player in the league. But Adams is also the kind of player just about anybody would want on his own team. Every team has players who can score. Not all of them have someone who can also make a difference without scoring.

Team executives voted Adams the NBA's toughest player in the 2018–19 NBA.com GM Survey, after he tied for the most votes the year before. The toughness he had to develop as a child would serve him well years later.

"He's proof that you don't have to talk the game. Just be tough," Clippers coach Doc Rivers said. "I like him as a player. I like what he stands for."

STEVEN ADAMS AT-A-GLANCE

BIRTHPLACE: Rotorua, New Zealand
BIRTH DATE: July 20, 1993
POSITION: Center
SIZE: 7'0", 265 pounds
TEAM: Oklahoma City Thunder
COLLEGE: Pittsburgh
DRAFTED: First round (No. 12 overall) in 2013

CHAPTER 2

GIANNIS ANTETOKOUNMPO

Giannis Antetokounmpo is from Greece, home of the Olympics, and he looks as if he could have been an Olympian in any number of sports.

When he dribbles from one end of the court to the other in just a few strides and leaps from around the foul line—which is 15 feet from the basket—he appears a natural for the long jump. And when he soars high above every other player and eventually the rim, 10 feet off the floor, for a slam dunk, he looks like he could have competed in the high jump.

Luckily for the Milwaukee Bucks, Antetokounmpo chose basketball as his sport—though not at first. He didn't particularly care for basketball as a boy. He wanted to be like his father and be a soccer player. He might've become a good one, but as a forward on

Giannis Antetokounmpo rises up for a basket during a 2019 game against the Washington Wizards.

the basketball court, he's on his way to becoming one of the greats.

Former teammate Matthew Dellavedova said of Antetokounmpo that "he really could be anything."

At 6-foot-11, Antetokounmpo is always one of the tallest players on the court. He looks even bigger with his arms spread because of his 7-foot-3 wingspan. But he's also so fast and such a good dribbler and passer that the Bucks began using him as their point guard, a position usually manned by players much shorter.

His unique combination of athleticism and skills earned him the nickname "The Greek Freak." It took him just a few years to develop his abilities enough to become not only an All-Star but also someone who would be considered a candidate for the NBA's Most Valuable Player (MVP) Award.

"He's an MVP candidate right now, and from what I saw, he'll definitely be in the (conversation) for the next decade or so," former teammate Greg Monroe said early in the 2017–18 season. "That's just the kind of player he is."

During the 2016–17 season, just his fourth in the league, Antetokounmpo became the first player in NBA history to rank in the league's top 20 in total points,

Antetokounmpo's scoring average increased in each of his first six seasons.

rebounds, assists, blocks, and steals. He also became one of only five players in the league's history to lead his team in per-game averages in those five categories.

It wasn't just his good basketball that made Antetokounmpo popular in Milwaukee. While many NBA players travel elsewhere during their summers to do their training, he spent his time in the city, where fans would see him visiting some of the same restaurants and stores that they did.

The journey that landed Antetokounmpo in Wisconsin was a long one. His parents moved from Nigeria to Greece, and Antetokounmpo has citizenship in both countries. His family was poor, but that would eventually change because of Giannis's basketball career.

Basketball is very popular in Greece, a country that has produced many players who became well known in Europe. When Greece beat the United States—a US team that included LeBron James, Dwyane Wade, Chris Paul, and Carmelo Anthony—in the semifinals of the 2006 world basketball championships, fans in Greece honked their horns and jumped out of their cars to celebrate in the streets.

Like many Greek players, Antetokounmpo started his career playing in that country's leagues and for its national team. He played in the Greek League All-Star Game in 2013 and also competed for Greece in the

Under-20 European Championships that year. By then it was clear his basketball future would move beyond Europe.

He wasn't drafted until the middle of the first round in the 2013 NBA Draft. Fans knew little about him when he first took the floor in his Bucks jersey, with his long last name stretching practically shoulder to shoulder across his back.

But Antetokounmpo quickly began compiling can't-miss highlights with his athletic plays. Even in a league with some of the best athletes in the

INTERNATIONAL COVER BOY

Antetokounmpo knew he had really made it to the big time when he made it to the cover of a video game. He was chosen for the cover of NBA 2K19, making him the first international player to earn that honor. Like many NBA players, Antetokounmpo said he enjoyed playing the popular game and said it was a dream to be chosen for the cover. The company said Antetokounmpo was the perfect choice as the first international choice. "Giannis is the future of the NBA, and his drive and athleticism have made him an undeniable force in the league," said Alfie Brody, NBA 2K's vice president of marketing.

world, he was doing things other players couldn't, and he became a fan favorite all over the world. He was elected to start in the All-Star Game for the first time in 2017, and two years later he received the most votes of any Eastern Conference player from fans. That made him a captain of one of the teams, along with James.

By then Antetokounmpo was one of the NBA's most dominant players and had helped turn the Bucks into one of its most dangerous teams. Milwaukee went on to put up the league's best record for the 2018–19 season at 60–22, and he was the only player in the league to average 25 points, 10 rebounds, and 5 assists. He had eye-popping stats like 17-for-21 shooting for 43 points in one game, and 27 points and 21 rebounds in another. And of the five Eastern Conference Player of the Month awards given out that season, Antetokounmpo won four.

The good times continued in the playoffs, as Antetokounmpo led the Bucks all the way to the conference finals. He led the team in points, rebounds, assists, and blocks per game, while tying for the team lead in steals per game.

The NBA, sensing what was to come, had scheduled the Bucks to play on Christmas that season for the first time since 1977. They visited the New York Knicks, and Antetokounmpo was so eager for the game that on his first shot attempt, he attempted a dunk. However, he was a little too pumped up and leaped so far off the court that he missed the basket with his slam and the ball rolled all the way to the corner.

"I was so excited that I went a little bit too high, and I thought the rim was a foot taller," Antetokounmpo said.

Spoken just like someone who could have been a high jumper.

GIANNIS ANTETOKOUNMPO
AT-A-GLANCE

BIRTHPLACE: Athens, Greece
BIRTH DATE: December 12, 1994
POSITION: Forward
SIZE: 6'11", 242 pounds
TEAM: Milwaukee Bucks
PREVIOUS TEAM: Filathlitikos, AO (Greece) (2012–13)
DRAFTED: First round (No. 15 overall) in 2013

CHAPTER 3

DEANDRE AYTON

The search for their next star player can send teams all around the globe. The Houston Rockets' quest took them to China for Yao Ming when they had the No. 1 draft pick in 2002. Many European countries have by now sent a player to the league.

For the Phoenix Suns, they didn't have to look far at all. Deandre Ayton was right there in their own state.

The Suns drafted Ayton in 2018, when they had the No. 1 pick for the first time in franchise history. He had spent his final two seasons of high school playing for Hillcrest Prep in Phoenix, and then went on to play one season of college basketball at Arizona in nearby Tucson. That made Ayton the NBA's first No. 1 pick ever to be drafted by a team in the same state where he played in both high school and college.

Deandre Ayton dunks on the Denver Nuggets during his rookie season.

That's exactly what Ayton had hoped for. He and his family had become fond of the area after having to move a couple of times first in pursuit of his basketball career.

"Everybody knows us now," he said shortly before the draft. "This is our second home, so we just feel welcome, and it would be a blessing if I become the No. 1 pick and stay here and make this home."

That's exactly what the Suns had in mind.

They had watched the 7-foot-1 Ayton develop into a versatile big man who was powerful enough to play near the basket but also quick enough to be effective away from it. He has a soft touch for someone so strong. That helps him shoot from the outside better than many players his size.

Ayton showed all of that during his one season at Arizona. He was the first player in the history of the Pac-12 Conference to be the league's Player of the Year, Freshman of the Year, and conference tournament MVP in the same season.

"There's nobody like Deandre," Arizona coach Sean Miller said. "Nobody."

Not long into his first NBA season, Ayton was already compiling dominating statistics, even against some of the toughest veterans in the game.

Over a three-game span in the middle of December, when he had been in the league only two months, Ayton averaged 25.0 points and 17.7 rebounds while making 71 percent of his shots. Then, at the end of that month, he had a game in which he went 16-for-20 from the floor and scored 33 points against a Denver team that was one of the best in the league.

AYTON'S ARRIVAL

Ayton helped beat one of college basketball's best teams when he was still in high school. He was playing for the Providence Storm, a team of players from the Bahamas, when North Carolina traveled there for a preseason exhibition tour in August 2014. Ayton, who had just turned 16 years old, had 17 points and 18 rebounds. His team surprised the Tar Heels 84–83. That performance made it clear that Ayton was one of basketball's best young prospects.

"That was one of the most fun games I've ever played in," Ayton said. "I was beating guys off the dribble, I was shooting jumpers, and I was grabbing rebounds over everyone."

Ayton averaged more than 16 points and 10 rebounds during his rookie season.

When he was drafted, Ayton became just the second player from the Bahamas to be a No. 1 draft pick. The first was Mychal Thompson, whose son Klay became an All-Star with the Golden State Warriors.

Like many NBA players who were born in another country, Ayton first had to come to the United States to fully develop his skills.

> **"YOU CAN FEEL GAME TO GAME HE IS GETTING BETTER. HE IS WORKING ON HIS GAME. HE IS A VERY DEDICATED PLAYER. IT WAS JUST A MATTER OF TIME."**
>
> —FORMER SUNS COACH IGOR KOKOSKOV

Basketball wasn't his focus as a child. It wasn't until he was 12, when he used $100 he earned working with his stepfather as a plumber to attend a basketball camp on the island, that basketball began to become a priority.

By that age he was already able to dunk, quite a feat for someone who wasn't even a teenager yet. Ayton moved to San Diego to go to school. He transferred to Phoenix for his final two seasons, where he was a teammate for one year at Hillcrest Prep with Marvin Bagley III. They would meet up again at the NBA Draft. Bagley was the No. 2 pick after Ayton.

Ayton's accomplishments as a rookie were a little obscured because of how well Luka Doncic, the No. 3 pick, was playing for Dallas. Plus, Ayton was often piling up points and rebounds in a losing effort, because the young Suns were one of the worst teams in the NBA.

But the Suns had no complaints. They could see how much effort Ayton was putting into improving, and they believed that would soon help their team improve as well.

"You can feel game to game he is getting better," then-Suns coach Igor Kokoskov said of Ayton in December of that year. "He is working on his game. He is a very dedicated player. It was just a matter of time."

Perhaps it would be only a matter of time until Ayton developed into an All-Star player and the Suns into a successful playoff team.

And they didn't even have to look far to find him.

DEANDRE AYTON AT-A-GLANCE

BIRTHPLACE: Nassau, Bahamas
BIRTH DATE: July 23, 1998
POSITION: Center
SIZE: 7'1", 250 pounds
TEAM: Phoenix Suns
COLLEGE: Arizona
DRAFTED: First round (No. 1 overall) in 2018

CHAPTER 4

DEVIN BOOKER

It's one thing to have a great night in the NBA. It's another to do it in Boston, home of the Celtics, the most storied and successful team in the league's history.

That's what Devin Booker did on March 24, 2017, when the Phoenix Suns shooting guard poured in 70 points, a total that had been reached by only five other players. None was as young as Booker, who was only 20 years old. Not even the great Michael Jordan ever scored 70 points. His best in one game was 69.

"Somehow I get reminded of it on a daily basis," Booker said. "I think because it happened in Boston, against the Celtics, one of the most historic franchises in the NBA, that added a little bit to it."

Devin Booker goes up for two of his 70 points against the Boston Celtics in 2017.

His 70-point game was big news everywhere the NBA is followed. Booker went to China the following summer, and people were calling him "Mr. 70."

His big numbers are hardly limited to one game, though.

Booker was only 21 years, 123 days old on March 2, 2018, when he reached 4,000 points for his career. Only LeBron James and Kevin Durant were younger when they reached that milestone.

Booker was limited to just 54 games in that 2017–18 season because of injuries and yet still scored 30 points on 22 occasions. That's a 30-point night every 2.5 games, which was second-best in the league.

Not bad for a guy who never even started a game in college.

Booker played on a powerhouse team in his lone season at Kentucky, one that won its first 38 games. In fact, the Wildcats were so loaded with talent that teammates Karl-Anthony Towns, Willie Cauley-Stein, and Trey Lyles had already been drafted by the time Booker was taken with the No. 13 pick in 2015.

So, he came off the bench in every one of his 38 games that season and was great as the sixth man, one of the most important roles in basketball. A team's top player who begins the game on the bench is counted on to help jump-start the squad if it isn't playing well or help increase the lead if the team is winning when he enters the game.

Booker was so successful at it that he was voted Sixth Man of the Year in the Southeastern Conference and was the Freshman of the Week in the conference five times. But it didn't take long in his NBA career to show that Booker was going to be a starter as a pro.

"Devin Booker (will) be the best player to ever wear the Phoenix Suns jersey," former Phoenix coach Earl Watson says he told friends after Booker's rookie season. "And I still believe it to this day."

> "DEVIN BOOKER (WILL) BE THE BEST PLAYER TO EVER WEAR THE PHOENIX SUNS JERSEY. AND I STILL BELIEVE IT TO THIS DAY."
>
> —EARL WATSON, FORMER SUNS COACH

His college coach didn't need convincing. Booker never started a game for John Calipari, but his early NBA success made the Wildcats coach think he should have reconsidered.

"Man, I held him back," Calipari wrote on his Twitter account, while encouraging fans to vote for Booker for the NBA All-Star Game on January 13, 2017.

Booker wasn't voted into that game but likely will have plenty of chances in the future. He has one of the best jump shots in the NBA, developed partly through workouts with his father, Melvin, who played parts of two seasons in the NBA and also played overseas. He was one of Devin's assistant coaches in high school after his own playing career ended.

And while his jumper has made Booker an elite scorer, he contributes much more than points for

SWEET SHOOTER

Booker competed in the three-point contest at the 2018 All-Star weekend and put up the best score in event history. He scored 28 points in the final round to beat Klay Thompson. Booker made 20 of his 25 shots in the round, including 4 out of 5 in his money-ball rack.

"Our season hasn't been too bright, so this is kind of a big deal back home," Booker said. "Hopefully, I can come back and win again. When I came out of college, I was just considered a shooter, but now I consider myself an elite shooter."

the Suns. He recorded his eighth career game with 35 points, five rebounds, and five assists in March 2019. That tied Gail Goodrich's team record.

Booker figured to have plenty of time to get that and many more Suns records. The Suns, wanting to make sure he would be on their team for years to come, signed him in the summer of 2018 to a maximum value contract extension worth $158 million.

His 70-point night in Boston was the highest total in the NBA since Kobe Bryant had scored 81 in 2006. Booker got to play against Bryant only once as a pro, as a 19-year-old on March 23, 2016. After the game, Bryant signed a pair of sneakers for Booker, writing on one of them: "To Book Be Legendary."

Booker might be on his way there.

DEVIN BOOKER AT-A-GLANCE

BIRTHPLACE: Grand Rapids, Michigan
BIRTH DATE: October 30, 1996
POSITION: Shooting Guard
SIZE: 6'6", 210 pounds
TEAM: Phoenix Suns
COLLEGE: Kentucky
DRAFTED: First round (No. 13 overall) in 2015

CHAPTER 5

CLINT CAPELA

The Houston Rockets under coach Mike D'Antoni were known for their love of the three-point shot. No team in NBA history had ever launched them more often than the Rockets. In the 2016–17 season, Houston set an NBA record by taking more than 3,300 attempts from behind the arc, an average of more than 40 per game.

The Rockets broke their own record the next season, taking more than 42 three-pointers per game, almost 3,500 for the season. In both seasons, they set league records for most three-pointers made.

All those three-point shots, and Clint Capela took only one.

Somebody had to do the work around the basket, and that became the 6-foot-10 Capela's job as he rose

While his teammates shoot three-pointers, Clint Capela does his best work under the basket.

from a little-known player who made little impact to an important contributor on one of the best teams in the league.

Capela, a center, averaged 13.9 points, 10.8 rebounds, and 1.85 blocks in 2017–18, all while playing only 27.5 minutes per game. He led the NBA in field-goal percentage, making 65.2 percent of his shots. He was second in the league in blocked shots and eighth in rebounding.

Even people who were around Capela all the time couldn't have predicted that after the way his career began.

> "IF YOU WOULD HAVE ASKED ME TWO YEARS AGO WOULD HE BE AT THIS LEVEL, I WOULD SAY NO, AND THAT WOULD BE A SURPRISE."
>
> –ROCKETS COACH MIKE D'ANTONI

"If you would have asked me two years ago would he be at this level, I would say no, and that would be a surprise," D'Antoni said. "Just his continued growth and just his energy level has gotten high."

"He has some talent, and he's getting better all the time."

Capela's improvement was one of the biggest reasons Houston was able to have the best record in the league, falling just one win short of making it all the way to the 2018 NBA Finals.

The Rockets had shooting guard James Harden, the league MVP, and had traded for Chris Paul, who had long been one of the best point guards in the NBA. And they had plenty of good outside shooters

DRIVING MORE THAN THE LANE

Capela wasn't just working on his game in his early years in the NBA. He was also working on how to get to the games. When he first arrived in Houston, he thought he would just walk from his home to the Rockets' arena. But the first time he did, he noticed nobody else was walking. He quickly understood why. "It is hot in Houston. It's a different level," he said. "By the time I made it to the arena and took my headphones off, and all this sweat pours out. It was like I went through a desert. And that's when I thought, 'Okay, I gotta get a driver's license.'" So, he learned to drive, though the first time he took the test, he backed his car into a barrier when he tried to parallel park. "Automatic fail," Capela said. He did pass on his next try.

who would station themselves around the three-point arc and try to capitalize when their playmakers got them open shots.

But teams couldn't focus entirely on stopping them because of how good Capela had become. Worry too much about what was happening on the outside, and Capela was likely to make them pay with two points on the inside.

"It's no secret everybody wants to always point out me and James, but he's the 'X' factor," Paul said.

That would have seemed unlikely just a few years earlier. Capela's skills were so limited in 2014–15, his rookie season, that he played in only 12 games. He spent much more time playing for the Rockets' team in the NBA Development League (now the G League).

Born in Geneva, Switzerland, Capela was playing for a team in France's top professional league before the Rockets drafted him with the No. 25 pick in the 2014 draft.

> **"IT'S NO SECRET EVERYBODY WANTS TO ALWAYS POINT OUT ME AND JAMES, BUT HE'S THE 'X' FACTOR."**
>
> **−ROCKETS POINT GUARD CHRIS PAUL**

Capela's strong inside game helps his teammates find more space to shoot on the perimeter.

The adjustment to a new home, and playing against the best basketball players in the world, was a tough one for Capela. He got off to such a bad start that he didn't make his first NBA basket until March 30, 2015. He had missed his first 11 shots of the season. He took

23 free throws that season and made only four, an incredibly low 17.4 percent.

"It just took me time to get comfortable: a new country, a new team, a new system," Capela said. "I was so impressed by everything—being in the NBA. I was just like, 'Wow.'"

But by his third season he was averaging in double figures, and in his fourth season he was the runner-up in the voting for the NBA's Most Improved Player Award. His statistics were on pace to increase again in numerous categories during the 2018–19 season before a right thumb injury forced Capela to miss a few weeks. Yet he still averaged a career-high 16.6 points and 12.7 rebounds in 67 games while helping lead the Rockets back to the playoffs. And once again, the Rockets took a record number of three-pointers, this time 3,721, with Capella accounting for none of them.

Before that season, Houston signed Capela

> "IT JUST TOOK ME TIME TO GET COMFORTABLE: A NEW COUNTRY, A NEW TEAM, A NEW SYSTEM. I WAS SO IMPRESSED BY EVERYTHING—BEING IN THE NBA. I WAS JUST LIKE, 'WOW.'"
>
> —CLINT CAPELA

to a contract that could pay him around $90 million. It was recognition of how important he had already become to the Rockets, and that he would be counted on even more in the future.

"Just because I know where I came from, I know how much work and focus that I've put into this," Capela said. "I've wanted to make myself important to the team. I'm just glad that now everybody sees it. It just gives me more motivation and confidence to continue what I'm doing."

And, perhaps someday, even make himself a three-point shooter.

CLINT CAPELA AT-A-GLANCE

BIRTHPLACE: Geneva, Switzerland
BIRTH DATE: May 18, 1994
POSITION: Center
SIZE: 6'10", 240 pounds
TEAM: Houston Rockets
PREVIOUS TEAM: Elan Chalon (France) (2012–14)
DRAFTED: First round (No. 25 overall) in 2014

CHAPTER 6

ANTHONY DAVIS

Anthony Davis stood just 6-foot-3 as he entered his junior year of high school in Chicago. At that age, some people have already reached their final height. If Davis had been one of them, perhaps he still would have gone on to the NBA, but it would have been as a guard.

Instead he had a growth spurt and grew 7 inches to 6-10 by the time he went to college. That allowed him to change positions and become a power forward. And not just any power forward. He's one of the best and most dominant ones in the game.

Davis rebounds and blocks shots as well as just about every other player his size. But because he had spent so much time playing as a guard, he maintained many of the shooting and dribbling skills of players

Anthony Davis rises up to block a shot against the Boston Celtics.

much shorter. So there really isn't anything Davis can't do on the court.

"I think he's the best player in the game," said Alvin Gentry, just a few months before taking over as Davis's coach in New Orleans in 2015. "There is nobody in the league I would trade him for. He's so talented that it's scary. To me, if you were starting your team today, he would be your No. 1 choice in the NBA."

> **"I THINK HE'S THE BEST PLAYER IN THE GAME. THERE IS NOBODY IN THE LEAGUE I WOULD TRADE HIM FOR. HE'S SO TALENTED THAT IT'S SCARY."**
>
> **—PELICANS COACH ALVIN GENTRY**

Few players can do as many things as Davis. He routinely is among the league leaders in points, rebounds, and blocked shots. During the 2016–17 season, he finished fourth in points per game, second in blocks, and seventh in rebounds. Only seven other players had finished in the top seven of all three categories in one season.

Even when he is having a big night scoring, Davis rarely neglects his other responsibilities to the team. He became only the second player in NBA history to have at least 40 points, 15 rebounds, and five steals in a game on more than one occasion. His ability to impact games on both offense and defense was so respected that in 2017–18 Davis finished in the top three in voting for both the MVP and Defensive Player of the Year awards.

But it was the feeling that he had to do perhaps too much that convinced Davis that he wanted to leave New Orleans and play elsewhere.

His agent told the Pelicans during the middle of the 2018–19 season that Davis wanted to be traded. Though the team had made the playoffs the previous season and even won its first-round series in a sweep, Davis believed that the Pelicans had failed to provide

STAR OF THE ALL-STARS

The NBA All-Star Game was played in New Orleans in 2017, which meant it would be Davis's night. If there was a player from the host city in the game, it was customary for the other All-Stars on his team to help him try for the MVP Award. His teammates on the Western Conference team did it perfectly, setting Davis up for easy shots that allowed him to score a record 52 points in the West's 192–182 victory.

"It was amazing," Davis said. "That's what I wanted to do."

Davis uses his immense size to overpower his opponents.

consistent enough help for him to be able to contend for championships in New Orleans.

"I gave the city, organization, fans everything I feel like I could," Davis said. "I don't know how long I'm going to play this game. People's careers are short, and I feel like it's my time to move on."

The Pelicans didn't trade him that February before the NBA's trading deadline, but there was no shortage

of interested teams. Interest in Davis hadn't always been so high, though.

He may have been a good player before his growth spurt, but there were many players like him or even better at that height. Once he shot up in size, though, he discovered that he could do so many more things, and colleges that had paid him little attention before were suddenly eager for Davis to come play for them.

"COMING IN TO THE OLYMPICS BEFORE HIS ROOKIE SEASON, THAT'S WHAT GUYS DREAM OF, AND TO DO IT AT 19, HE'S GOING TO BE A PHENOMENAL PLAYER, MAN."

—KEVIN DURANT, OLYMPIC TEAMMATE

"It makes the game a whole lot easier," Davis said. "Rebounding, blocking shots, and shooting over guys. If you're 6-3, when you go in the hole, you're going over guys and getting your shot blocked. When you're 6-10, you can go up and dunk on someone. To also have the ability to shoot the ball, I'd rather be 6-10."

Davis ended up choosing Kentucky, one of the best college programs. He led the Wildcats to the 2012 national championship in his lone season and won most of the national player of the year awards. After that season, he entered the NBA Draft, and New Orleans took him with the No. 1 pick.

Before playing his first NBA game, he was picked for the US team that was going to London for the 2012 Olympics. The Americans had been using NBA players almost exclusively in the Olympics for 20 years, and Davis became only the third player since 1992 to go straight from college to the red, white, and blue uniform of Team USA.

"Coming in to the Olympics before his rookie season, that's what guys dream of, and to do it at 19, he's going to be a phenomenal player, man," teammate Kevin Durant said. "He's going to be one of those guys who changes a franchise for decades."

ANTHONY DAVIS AT-A-GLANCE

BIRTHPLACE: Chicago, Illinois
BIRTH DATE: March 11, 1993
POSITION: Forward–Center
SIZE: 6'10", 253 pounds
TEAM: New Orleans Pelicans
COLLEGE: Kentucky
DRAFTED: First round (No. 1 overall) in 2012

CHAPTER 7

LUKA DONCIC

Many players expecting to be picked high in the NBA Draft spend the days before it in New York. That's where the draft is held, and there are many things for them to do beforehand. They can go shopping at some of the city's famous stores for the suit they will wear on draft night. They can meet with people from sneaker companies or other businesses they may endorse, or attend events where they can meet fans.

Luka Doncic had other plans.

The shooting guard was in Spain, leading his team to a European pro basketball championship. By the time he was drafted on a Thursday night, he'd already had an amazing week.

An amazing year, actually, filled with championships for his teams and his country.

Luka Doncic dribbles around a Charlotte Hornets defender in a 2019 game.

Doncic led all rookies in points per game in 2018–19.

"It's like a dream," Doncic said. "I've been dreaming about being a EuroLeague champion, being a European team champion, being drafted. All this year has been like a dream."

And at age 19, he was just getting started.

Doncic began his NBA career for the Dallas Mavericks just like he finished his European one, by taking and making big shots against much older players and winning over fans all over the world because of the way he played.

The Mavericks had one of the greatest international players in NBA history in Dirk Nowitzki of Germany, and they believed Doncic, who was born in Slovenia, could be the next one. But it was going to be unlikely they could get him in the 2018 draft, because they had only the No. 5 pick, and Doncic wasn't expected to last that long. So, the Mavericks arranged a trade with the Atlanta Hawks, who were at No. 3. They swapped spots, with Dallas also having to send the Hawks another first-round pick in the future. That's a lot to give up for a player who hadn't played in an NBA game, but the Mavericks were sure it was a move worth making.

"It was meticulously thought out," coach Rick Carlisle said. "We gave up something of value, but it was well calculated as to the reward versus risk."

It didn't take long for Doncic to start rewarding the Mavericks for their confidence in him.

Dallas put him right in the starting lineup, and he scored 20 or more points in 13 of his first 25 games. That set a record for a teenager, after both Kevin Durant and Kyrie Irving had done it 12 times in their first 25 games. Doncic was voted the Western Conference Rookie of the Month for October/November, and then he went on to win the award the next four months, too, as he started to appear in the highlights more and more often.

One night it was for scoring 11 straight points late in a game to beat Houston. Another night it was for becoming the first teenager to make seven three-pointers in a game, scoring 34 points in a thriller against New Orleans.

"It's pretty clear that he's got a flair for the moment," Carlisle said after the victory over the Rockets. "He's unafraid. You don't see that every day."

LAST HIGHLIGHT IN EUROPE

The last big shot of Doncic's European career was one most players wouldn't even try. With Real Madrid clinging to a three-point lead over Baskonia and the shot clock running down in Game 4 of the ACB Championship series, the ball came out to Doncic on the perimeter. He took one dribble, then launched a three-pointer off one leg as he was drifting backward. The shot went in for a six-point lead with 2:40 left. His team went on to win 96–85 to cap off the series and that portion of his career. "It has been the season of my life," Doncic said. "It's incredible."

Actually, fans across Europe had seen it for quite a while by then.

Doncic had signed with Real Madrid in Spain, one of Europe's best-known teams, when he was just 13 years old. Before long he was a key player, and in 2017-18 he put together a season that had rarely been seen.

Real Madrid won the EuroLeague title in 2018, when Doncic became the youngest MVP of both the EuroLeague and its Final Four. Then, Real Madrid won its Spanish League championship in June, with Doncic winning MVP honors for that as well. Luckily for Doncic, they wrapped up the series in four games, so he could get on a plane and get to New York in time for the draft. Had the series gone to a fifth game, he would've had to miss his NBA introduction.

Despite all those titles and awards, not to mention helping win Slovenia's first European championship in 2017, there were still skeptics. There had been just enough European players who were drafted high but didn't last long in the NBA to make people wonder if Doncic could really be worth the hype.

Others needed no further convincing.

"He may be the most accomplished European teenager to ever come into the draft," ESPN draft analyst Jay Bilas said. "You know, there's very little that is unknown about him. He's not some workout wonder that people are projecting. He's accomplished things, and he has been seen in five-on-five against high-level competition for a number of years. He's played professional basketball since he was 13."

After he averaged 21.2 points, 7.8 rebounds, and six assists as a rookie, Doncic looks like he'll be playing for many more years. Few players had ever matched Doncic's accomplishments in Europe, and he did it all before he turned 20. Mavericks fans can't wait to see everything he can do in the NBA.

LUKA DONCIC AT-A-GLANCE

BIRTHPLACE: Ljubljana, Slovenia

BIRTH DATE: February 28, 1999

POSITION: Shooting Guard

SIZE: 6'7", 218 pounds

TEAM: Dallas Mavericks

PREVIOUS TEAM: Real Madrid (Spain) (2015–18)

DRAFTED: First round (No. 3 overall) by the Atlanta Hawks in 2018

CHAPTER 8

JOEL EMBIID

From 2013 through 2016, the Philadelphia 76ers were the worst team in the NBA. At one point, they set the record for the longest losing streak in league history, with 28 consecutive losses. In 2015–16 they won only 10 games and lost 72, only one loss away from tying for the most ever.

It wasn't simply a matter of bad luck, or that good players suddenly stopped playing up to their potential. Being bad was part of the 76ers' plan. By losing lots of games, they would be able to replenish their roster with high draft picks. Fans of the team seemed to understand the strategy, which even earned the nickname "the Process."

"Trust the Process," Joel Embiid said.

Joel Embiid brought hope back to the Philadelphia 76ers.

It led to the 76ers getting Embiid, so why wouldn't they?

But even Embiid's emergence required some patience. Though he had started playing the game only a few years earlier in Cameroon, where he grew up, Embiid was the No. 3 pick in the 2014 draft. That alone spoke to his potential. Unfortunately for the 76ers, they would have to wait a while to see him play. He missed what would have been his first two NBA seasons, 2014–15 and 2015–16, because of foot injuries, so he didn't actually debut in the league until October 2016.

In his long-awaited first game, Embiid scored 20 points against the Oklahoma City Thunder and soon appeared well on his way to winning Rookie of the Year. He was the Eastern Conference Rookie of the Month for November, December, and January, and was averaging 20.2 points, 7.8 rebounds, and 2.5 blocks. Then injuries struck again. Embiid tore his meniscus in his left knee during a January game, spelling the end of his season.

This led to an intense debate when it came time for voting for the Rookie of the Year Award. Embiid had clearly been the best player, and his team was doing well when he was healthy. But he had played in only 31 games, meaning he missed more than 50.

In the end, voters decided that wasn't enough. They voted Milwaukee's Malcolm Brogdon the winner, and Embiid wasn't even the highest-finishing player on the 76ers. Dario Saric was second, while Embiid had to settle for third place.

That didn't affect how the 76ers thought about him. Before the next season, they signed him to a five-year contract extension.

FOR EMBIID, IT'S BEST TO BE BOLD

Because of Embiid's injuries, the 76ers were cautious about how much they would use him. Sometimes that meant not playing him in one game if they played on two straight nights, or having him not take part in practice. But Embiid prefers to be bold. When he leaped over the first row of fans to try to save a ball in a game against the Knicks, 76ers coach Brett Brown said he would rather his franchise center wouldn't take such risks. But Embiid made it clear that's not his style. "I only know one way to play, and that's to play hard and compete," he said.

Embiid helped the 76ers become one of the top teams in the Eastern Conference.

The Process was paying off. The Process even became a nickname for Embiid, and fans would chant "Trust the Process!" when he was shooting free throws. And once Embiid was able to play, it wasn't long before the 76ers started winning again.

Returning to the court in 2017–18, Embiid averaged 22.9 points and 11 rebounds. And he did so while teaming up with rookie Ben Simmons to form a 1–2 punch of big man and point guard that catapulted the 76ers to 52 wins. The Sixers not only returned to the playoffs for the first time in six years but even reached the second round.

Finally able to play in the majority of his team's games, Embiid was voted to the All-Defensive second team that season. But beyond the rebounds and blocked shots expected from a 7-footer, he also flashed the skills of a player much smaller. He averaged 3.2 assists, which is a lot for a big man, and in a game against the Los Angeles Lakers early that season finished with 46 points, 15 rebounds, seven assists, and seven blocked shots. That marked the most points scored by a 76ers player in 11 years, and it was the first time since 1982 that an NBA player scored 40 points while also getting seven assists and seven blocks.

"Tonight we realized we had Joel Embiid, and he was just dominant," 76ers coach Brett Brown said after that game.

Embiid continued his emergence in 2018–19. Playing in a career-high 64 games, Embiid also averaged a career-high 27.5 points and 13.6 rebounds while being selected as an All-Star Game starter for the second straight year. Just as important, though, was that the Sixers were starting to become really good. Just three years after winning a dismal 10 games, Philadelphia posted its second consecutive 50-win season in 2018–19, and then the team won a series for the second year in a row.

Things were finally looking up for Embiid and the 76ers, though it wasn't just his lofty statistics that made him so popular. He had been well known for his humorous social media posts from even before he started playing, and he would often end his postings on Twitter with the hashtag #TheProcess.

He would taunt opponents, sometimes posting photos of himself dunking on one, cheer for his favorite teams, or sometimes even poke fun at himself. Most important to 76ers fans, he would occasionally use his posts to back the team or the city.

The 76ers' losing strategy had bothered people who disagreed with it, feeling that a team should always do its best to win. Critics enjoyed rubbing it in when things didn't go the Sixers' way, such as at the 2017 draft lottery, when Philadelphia had a chance of getting two picks in the top four but ended up with only the No. 3 pick. Embiid, who represented the team onstage, quickly put a positive spin on things.

"I wish we would have gotten the No. 1 pick," he said, "but we trust the process, and it's going to be exciting to see what we're going for."

After all, the process was paying off, and with Embiid leading the way, the Sixers were on the way to becoming an Eastern Conference power.

JOEL EMBIID AT-A-GLANCE

BIRTHPLACE: Yaounde, Cameroon
BIRTH DATE: March 16, 1994
POSITION: Center
SIZE: 7'0", 260 pounds
TEAM: Philadelphia 76ers
COLLEGE: Kansas
DRAFTED: First round (No. 3 overall) in 2014

CHAPTER 9

AARON GORDON

Imagine trying to make a basket and having a dragon in your way. A tall, green dragon with a snout for a nose who is standing on top of a hoverboard.

Aaron Gordon simply jumped over him.

That was during the Slam Dunk Contest during the NBA's All-Star weekend in 2016. Gordon didn't win the contest that night in Toronto, but he had some of the most memorable slams the event has ever seen.

Iconic players such as Michael Jordan and Kobe Bryant have been slam-dunk champions, but nobody had ever attempted anything quite like what Gordon did. The dunk began with some help from Stuff the Magic Dragon, the Orlando Magic's mascot. With Stuff spinning around on a hoverboard with the ball, Gordon grabbed it with one hand and did a 360-degree dunk.

Aaron Gordon flies high over the Orlando Magic mascot during the 2016 NBA Dunk Contest.

On his next dunk, he got another assist from Stuff. Gordon leaped high to take the ball, put it under his legs—while nearly in a sitting position in midair—and slammed it down with his left hand.

Both dunks earned a perfect score of 50 points from the five judges. Many people thought Gordon should have won. However, Zach LaVine held Gordon off in a final-round "dunk-off."

"I knew I wanted to do that because it was just different. I knew it hadn't been done in the NBA dunk contest," Gordon said. "I knew all four of my initial dunks hadn't been done in the NBA dunk contest before."

He may be best known for that contest, but it would be wrong to think of Gordon as just a dunker. The 6-foot-9 forward has worked hard on his shot every year he's been in the NBA. In his fourth season, Gordon had a game in which he went 5-for-5 on three-pointers while scoring 41 points. That was the highest total of his career.

That's right, able to dunk over dragons and fire in three-pointers.

Gordon had two 40-point games in that 2017–18 season. No Orlando player had done that in seven seasons.

"He's got a chance to be one of the more complete players in the NBA," teammate Arron Afflalo said during that season.

Gordon is part of an athletic family. His father, older brother, and sister all played college basketball, and it soon became clear Aaron was going to do the same. He was twice California's Mr. Basketball in high school, and as a senior in 2013 was the MVP of the McDonald's All-American Game. Later that summer, he

GORDON PLAYS THE BAD GUY

Gordon had a role in the movie *Uncle Drew* in 2018, and part of it came naturally. He was the high-flying Casper Jones, a powerful dunker who was the best player on his team. But unlike in real life, where his dunks made him a fan favorite, he was the bad guy on screen. He was the trash-talking rival who played against the team that included Kyrie Irving, Shaquille O'Neal, and Chris Webber. "I'm the nicest villain that you'll ever meet in your life," Gordon said. "Toward the end of the movie, you're like, 'I don't really like this guy, and I'm happy he gets what he deserves.' But I think I played the part pretty well. If I need to play the villain, then I can play the villain."

Gordon dunks against the Brooklyn Nets in 2018.

led the United States to the gold medal in the under-19 world championships, winning that MVP award, too.

NBA success didn't come quite so quickly.

He was the No. 4 pick in the 2014 draft after one season at Arizona, but he missed almost half his first season because of injuries and averaged only 5.2 points. He averaged less than 10 points per game the next season, too. But by his fourth season he increased that all the way to 17.6 points.

The Magic didn't make the playoffs in any of those years, but Gordon was hopeful for the future.

"It would be a beautiful thing to go from one of the worst teams in the league to one of the best," Gordon said. "It would be a beautiful story."

That story began to change for the Magic in 2018–19, when the team won 42 games and reached the playoffs for the first time in seven seasons. Gordon, for his part, scored 16 points and dished out a career-high 3.7 assists per game. That was the kind of output the Magic were hoping for when they signed him to a new four-year contract prior to that season.

AARON GORDON AT-A-GLANCE

BIRTHPLACE: San Jose, California
BIRTH DATE: September 16, 1995
POSITION: Forward
SIZE: 6'9", 220 pounds
TEAM: Orlando Magic
COLLEGE: Arizona
DRAFTED: First round (No. 4 overall) in 2014

CHAPTER 10

NIKOLA JOKIC

Nikola Jokic is 7 feet tall and weighs 250 pounds, and a player that size has almost always played a certain way. He would wait near the basket for someone to pass him the ball. It was rare that someone so big and tall was the one who would do the passing to others.

But that's the way Jokic plays.

He is such a good passer that he calls himself a point guard trapped in a center's body, except nobody believes it but him. But watch the Denver Nuggets star play, and there's no reason to argue.

"He used to be a fat point guard," Denver coach Michael Malone said. "He was a point guard growing up. He had the ball in his hands. That's why I think his ball handling, his passing are where they're at because he has that foundation growing up."

Nikola Jokic averaged a career-high 7.3 assists per game in 2018–19.

That's not to say that Jokic is just a passer.

He still does the scoring and rebounding that's expected of someone his size, and many times he does all three things in the same game. By the time he was 23 years old, Jokic already had 20 triple-doubles, with 10 or more points, rebounds, and assists in the same game. Only Oscar Robertson and Magic Johnson, two of the best guards ever, were younger when they reached that total. Both were 22.

It wasn't that Jokic was particularly athletic, allowing him to accumulate his impressive statistics through talent alone. He had to use his smarts just as much as strength or speed.

"He's kind of pudgy," San Antonio Spurs coach Gregg Popovich joked. "He doesn't jump out of the gym. He doesn't run that fast, but he might be one of the smartest players in the league. And he's got skills and he knows how to use them, and he enjoys the (heck) out of himself out there. He's been very important for them, obviously."

Jokic is from Serbia, and his style is similar to the way European big men have played. The focus there is often on teamwork more than talent, and that means everyone has to be able to pass and shoot from the outside, not just the guards.

That's how centers such as Vlade Divac and Arvydas Sabonis became such good passers a generation earlier. They were so good that sometimes their teams would pass the ball to them not so they would shoot, but so they would deliver a pass to someone else for an open shot.

With his height and vision, Jokic is able to look over the top of the defense and find teammates who are cutting to the basket for a layup or popping away from

PASSION FOR THE TRACK

Jokic is a big man even by basketball standards. Imagine him by horse racing standards. That sport became Jokic's other passion, along with basketball, when he was a teenager growing up in Serbia. He got into basketball because his two older brothers played it. "But then at some point in my life I started to go into horse racing," Jokic said. "I just fell in love with horses and their beauty and elegance." He liked to work in the stable with the horses who competed in harness racing, though he did finish fourth once when he got onto the track to do the racing himself. Jokic liked horses so much that he eventually became an owner. His horse, Dream Catcher, got its first win in 2017, when Malone was in Serbia to visit Jokic over the summer.

Jokic goes up for a basket against the Los Angeles Lakers.

it for a jump shot. By his fourth season, Jokic already had more than 30 games in which he dished out 10 or more assists. Among centers, only Wilt Chamberlain finished with more in NBA history.

Sometimes the Nuggets needed Jokic to handle more of the scoring load himself, and he has delivered multiple 40-point games. It has been a rapid rise for

a player who wasn't necessarily seen as a superstar to be.

Jokic was only the No. 41 pick in the 2014 draft, an unusually low spot for a player who became an All-Star. He spent one more season playing for his team in Serbia and then made an impact right away when he joined the Nuggets, averaging 10 points and getting

> **"NIKOLA EMBODIES EVERYTHING WE LOOK FOR IN A PLAYER AND PERSON AS HE WILL DO ANYTHING ASKED OF HIM BECAUSE HIS ONLY CONCERN IS HELPING HIS TEAM WIN."**
>
> —JOSH KROENKE, NUGGETS TEAM PRESIDENT

voted to the All-Rookie first team. After that season, he helped Serbia win the silver medal in the 2016 Olympics in Rio de Janeiro, Brazil.

He really took off the next season, when he had both his first 40-point game and his first triple-double. Jokic finished with averages of 16.7 points, 9.8 rebounds, and 4.9 assists that season, and he was the runner-up to Giannis Antetokounmpo for the 2017 Most Improved Player Award. Then he upped his averages in all three stats in 2017–18.

Though they hadn't reached the playoffs yet since his arrival, the Nuggets knew they needed Jokic to get there. They gave him a contract extension worth almost $150 million in the summer of 2018, even though they didn't need to commit to that for another year and could have saved a lot of money by waiting.

"Nikola embodies everything we look for in a player and person as he will do anything asked of him because his only concern is helping his team win," said Josh Kroenke, Denver's team president. "Seeing Nikola grow on and off the basketball court is something in which our organization has taken immense pride, and we were determined to do whatever it took to keep Nikola in a Nuggets uniform for a very long time."

The Nuggets' bet quickly paid off, as Jokic again set career highs for average points, rebounds, and assists in 2017–18, while also being selected for his first All-Star Game. More important for Jokic, though, he helped Denver post the second-best record in the Western Conference and reach the playoffs for the first time in six seasons.

NIKOLA JOKIC AT-A-GLANCE

BIRTHPLACE: Sombor, West Backa, Serbia
BIRTH DATE: February 19, 1995
POSITION: Center
SIZE: 7'0", 250 pounds
TEAM: Denver Nuggets
PREVIOUS TEAM: KK Mega Vizura (Serbia) 2012–15
DRAFTED: Second round (No. 41 overall) in 2014

CHAPTER 11

DONOVAN MITCHELL

Much of the focus on Donovan Mitchell's first season in the NBA was on a race he wouldn't win. He ultimately fell short in the voting for Rookie of the Year, finishing as the runner-up to Ben Simmons.

Perhaps it's better to focus on everything Mitchell did do in 2017–18.

No rookie that season averaged more than his 20.5 points per game. No first-year player had ever made more than his 187 three-pointers. Throw in a trip to the second round of the playoffs and a Slam Dunk Contest championship, and it was an extraordinary season, even if the panel of voters who cover the NBA favored Simmons's accomplishments.

Even Mitchell couldn't have seen everything turning out so well.

Donovan Mitchell's huge rookie season helped the Jazz reach the second round of the 2018 playoffs.

The Utah Jazz had only a 19–28 record in the middle of January, and Mitchell worried that he wasn't doing enough to help his team win.

"There would be nights where I just couldn't fall asleep," said Mitchell, a shooting guard. "I'd just be in bed and couldn't sleep because I was thinking about it. This is crazy how all this has come together, to be honest."

Simmons ended up winning the rookie award rather easily. He received 90 first-place votes compared with only 11 for Mitchell in a race that many people thought would be much closer. But voting was done at the end of the regular season. If playoff performance had been considered, perhaps the results would have been different.

> "DONOVAN IS THE TRUTH AND HE'S ONLY GOING TO GET BETTER, WHICH IS SCARY FOR THE LEAGUE. YOU HAVE TO KNOW WHERE HE'S AT ALL THE TIME. HE'S SPECIAL."
>
> —GOLDEN STATE WARRIORS FORWARD DRAYMOND GREEN

That's when Mitchell really showed how good he was. He helped the Jazz engineer a first-round upset of the Oklahoma City Thunder, who had the reigning NBA MVP in Russell Westbrook, along with superstars Paul George and Carmelo Anthony. Utah lost in the second round to the Houston Rockets, but not before Mitchell had one of the best playoff debuts that had been seen in some time.

"Donovan is the truth and he's only going to get better, which is scary for the league," Golden State star Draymond Green said. "You have to know where he's at all the time. He's special."

THE PLAYERS' CHOICE

Mitchell may have fallen short in the Rookie of the Year voting, but he wasn't completely shut out of the awards for first-year players. The National Basketball Players Association had begun awarding its own honors, voted on by the players. They called their award the "Leader of the New School," given to a player who rose to the occasion and proved he was a star in the making. They gave it to Mitchell, allowing him to more easily accept not winning the more famous award from the media. "But I won the award from my peers, so I don't care what analysts think. They're not the ones who have to guard me," Mitchell said during an appearance on fellow player J J Redick's podcast.

Mitchell quickly established himself as a key player for the Jazz.

Mitchell averaged 24.4 points in the postseason and became just the fourth rookie to score 200 points in his first eight playoff games. Only Kareem Abdul-Jabbar—the leading scorer in NBA history—Wilt Chamberlain, and Elgin Baylor had done that.

By then, Mitchell had already proven he had a knack for being a fast starter. He scored 14 points in

his first game in college at Louisville. That made him one of only 10 players in school history to score that many in his first game as a freshman.

Still, what he did as an NBA rookie would have been tough to predict when he was drafted. Mitchell was considered a good prospect but not one of the best at his position. By the time he was taken with the

No. 13 pick by the Denver Nuggets, who traded his rights to the Jazz, a number of guards had already been selected. New York (Frank Ntilikina), Dallas (Dennis Smith Jr.), and Charlotte (Malik Monk) all could have considered Mitchell with picks ranging from No. 8 to No. 11, but they opted for other backcourt players.

Mitchell ended up outshining them and just about every other player from his class. Simmons wasn't actually in that draft class. He was drafted the year before but sat out his first season with an injury. That made him eligible for the Rookie of the Year Award the next year, when he could start playing, even though it was really his second season in the league.

Mitchell is only 6-foot-3, which isn't tall for an NBA player. But he makes up for that with excellent athleticism that allowed him to also play goalkeeper in soccer and shortstop and pitcher in baseball in high school.

The player whose nickname is "Spider" climbed high to overcome his height and win the Slam Dunk Contest at his first All-Star weekend. There were many more highlights during that season, when he became only the fifth rookie in 60 years to be the leading scorer on a team that won at least 45 games.

The trick would be keeping it up as defenses became more familiar with him. That wasn't a problem, as Mitchell kept right on going in his second season, scoring more points than any other Utah player in his first 100 games with the team. He also improved his averages in scoring, assists, and rebounds in 2018–19, while leading Utah back to the playoffs.

The 2018 Rookie of the Year Award had eluded Mitchell. But many more awards seem on the way in the future.

"You can ride the wave and be complacent. I've never been that way," Mitchell said.

DONOVAN MITCHELL
AT-A-GLANCE

BIRTHPLACE: Elmsford, New York
BIRTH DATE: September 7, 1996
POSITION: Shooting Guard
SIZE: 6'3", 215 pounds
TEAM: Utah Jazz
COLLEGE: Louisville
DRAFTED: First round (No. 13 overall) by the Denver Nuggets in 2017

CHAPTER 12

BEN SIMMONS

Ben Simmons has raced from Down Under right toward the top of the NBA. The No. 1 draft pick after one year of college. The NBA's 2017–18 Rookie of the Year. An All-Star in just his second pro season. Simmons plays fast, and his accolades are piling up just as quickly.

"He puts his thumbprint on a game immediately with his athleticism and his size," 76ers coach Brett Brown said. "He can rebound and run and create and get to the rim. He has been doing this at historic proportions."

At 6-foot-10, Simmons has the height of a forward but the speed of a guard. The 76ers list him as both positions, because he can easily transition from one to the other depending on who else is in the game.

With his unique skill set, Ben Simmons quickly rose up the ranks to become one of the NBA's biggest stars.

At his size, Simmons is able to grab defensive rebounds and then quickly push the ball up the floor for fast breaks. That gives the 76ers an advantage over many teams, who usually need to have the player who grabbed the rebound pass it to someone else to dribble the ball into the front court. LeBron James even called Simmons a "one-man fast break" because of his ability to do that.

Simmons quickly drew comparisons to hall of famer Magic Johnson, who was another tall and versatile guard. The comparison seemed especially fitting in 2018, after Simmons became the first rookie since Johnson in 1980 to record a triple-double in the postseason. Before that, Simmons had 12 triple-doubles during the 2017–18 regular season. Only Oscar Robertson, another hall of famer and the career leader in triple-doubles, had more as a rookie. Robertson finished with 26 in 1960–61. It was a dominant debut for a player who grew up in an emerging basketball country.

Simmons was born in Australia, where his father played professional basketball. As a kid, the younger Simmons showed great ability. Eventually it became obvious he was too good for the competition back in his home country, so he moved to the United States in high school.

He played one season at Louisiana State (LSU), where his averages of 19.2 points, 11.8 rebounds, and 4.8 assists all ranked in the top five in the Southeastern Conference. Simmons was the leading rebounder among all Division I freshmen and was honored with a number of Freshman of the Year awards following the season.

The 76ers then selected Simmons with the top pick in the 2016 draft, their first No. 1 pick since Allen Iverson in 1996. However, they had to wait longer than they hoped to actually see him on the court.

A STAR BACK HOME

Brett Brown has history in Australia. He was a coach on one of the teams Simmons's father, David, played for in Australia's National Basketball League. He also coached Australia's Olympic team, which was still searching for its first medal. Before the 2018–19 season, Brown returned to the country and noticed Ben Simmons on a giant billboard in a plaza in Melbourne, and children wearing his No. 25 jerseys or 76ers hats all over. "They love basketball," Brown said. "I think his impact is significant. It is far-reaching."

Simmons's play as a rookie helped the 76ers reach the playoffs for the first time in six years.

Simmons broke a bone in his right foot during training camp. He was originally expected to return sometime during the season. Fans kept waiting and waiting. The 76ers eventually announced that the injury wasn't healing the way they had hoped and that Simmons would miss the entire season.

Simmons was disappointed that he couldn't play but vowed to use the time to work on his game.

"My time will come," he said.

It came pretty quickly.

Simmons went right into the starting lineup in 2017–18 and showed that neither his injury nor inactivity had slowed him down. He ended up joining Robertson as the only rookies in NBA history to average at least 15 points, eight rebounds, and eight assists, and he was voted the Rookie of the Year.

Critics argued that Simmons shouldn't have been eligible for the award because it was actually his second season in the league. But because he didn't play in the first season, he was still considered a rookie when he did finally take the floor. He ended up easily beating out Utah's Donovan Mitchell to become the third player in 76ers history to win the award.

While the individual award was nice, Philadelphia fans were more excited by finally seeing team success again.

The 76ers hadn't made the playoffs since 2012 and had become one of the worst teams in the NBA. They finally got back to the postseason in 2018, and Simmons's play was a major reason why.

Philadelphia won its final 16 games of the regular season to finish with a 52–30 record. All-Star center Joel Embiid had broken a bone in his face during that stretch and had to sit out until the playoffs, but the 76ers didn't slow down at all, because of how well Simmons played.

Though they lost to the Boston Celtics in the second round, the 76ers were positioning themselves for another playoff run the next season. They made trades during the season to acquire veterans Jimmy Butler and Tobias Harris. With that group, Philadelphia won 51 games and went into the playoffs as the third seed in the Eastern Conference, where the team again advanced to the second round.

Simmons, despite being in just his second season and still not being a fully polished outside shooter, was often counted on not only to provide his own offense but also to get all the veterans the ball as well. He was eager for the challenge.

"We're in a good position," Simmons said.

BEN SIMMONS AT-A-GLANCE

BIRTHPLACE: Melbourne, Australia
BIRTH DATE: July 20, 1996
POSITION: Guard-Forward
SIZE: 6'10", 230 pounds
TEAM: Philadelphia 76ers
COLLEGE: Louisiana State
DRAFTED: First round (No. 1 overall) in 2016

CHAPTER 13

JAYSON TATUM

In May 2017, the Boston Celtics won the NBA's Draft Lottery. That gave them the right to pick first in the next month's draft. Then, just days before the draft, the Celtics traded the pick to the Philadelphia 76ers. The teams swapped spots in the order, which meant the Celtics were agreeing to drop to the No. 3 spot.

It was a risky move that is rarely done. Many teams wouldn't even consider it. After all, who would want to risk giving up the opportunity to pick the player who would be considered the best talent available? But for Danny Ainge, the Celtics' president of basketball operations, the move made sense.

"We think there's a really good chance the player that we'll take at three was the same player we would have taken at one," Ainge explained.

The Boston Celtics' faith in Jayson Tatum paid off when he developed into a star.

Tatum goes up for a contested shot against the Philadelphia 76ers.

That player ended up being Jayson Tatum.

The 76ers went on to use that No. 1 pick on Markelle Fultz. He ended up being injured a lot and made little impact before the 76ers traded him during his second season. Meanwhile, Tatum nearly led the Celtics to the NBA Finals in his first season.

It was a remarkable and surprising run. The Celtics had lost Kyrie Irving and Gordon Hayward, considered their top two veteran players, to season-ending injuries. Yet Tatum played so well that Boston made it all the way to the Eastern Conference Finals before losing to the Cleveland Cavaliers in Game 7.

Tatum scored 351 points in the postseason, only one fewer than Kareem Abdul-Jabbar's record for most by a rookie. And he earned the respect of Cavaliers star LeBron James for the way he played and acted for someone who was only 20 years old.

> "I JUST LOVE EVERYTHING ABOUT THE KID. THE WAY HE PLAYS THE GAME, HIS DEMEANOR, WHERE HE COMES FROM. I KNOW HIS PARENTS, AND I KNOW HE'S BUILT FOR STARDOM. HE'S BUILT FOR SUCCESS, AND THAT'S ON AND OFF THE FLOOR."
>
> —LOS ANGELES LAKERS STAR LEBRON JAMES

"I just love everything about the kid," James said. "The way he plays the game, his demeanor, where he comes from. I know his parents, and I just know he's built for stardom. He's built for success, and that's on and off the floor."

James and Tatum had met years earlier. Tatum's godfather, Larry Hughes, had been a teammate of James's, and Jayson went to the superstar's basketball camp when he was younger. Tatum apparently learned plenty there and elsewhere while growing up to make him one of the top prospects in the country.

Growing up in St. Louis, Tatum became the Gatorade national high school player of the year and an All-American. Tatum chose to play college ball at Duke, where he spent one season before entering the draft.

Tatum hoped to be the No. 1 pick, but the Celtics were right that they were able to get him at No. 3. Ainge would say after the draft that Tatum was the player he planned to pick all along.

"There's a lot to like about Jayson," Ainge said. "He's going to be a terrific player."

TATUM AND THE TRADE TALKS

Just as he was settling in as the potential star of the future in Boston, Tatum had to deal with reports that he may not be there for long. When Anthony Davis requested a trade from New Orleans in the middle of Tatum's second NBA season, there was speculation that the Celtics would try to make an offer in the summer. If they did, it was expected they would have to agree to include Tatum in the package. Yet Tatum didn't react angrily, telling Celtics radio color commentator Cedric Maxwell that "I'd trade me too for Anthony Davis."

Tatum began to show that from his very first NBA game.

Boston began that season at Cleveland, and the season started on a sad note. Hayward, the star forward the Celtics had signed during the summer, broke his leg just a few minutes into the game. He wouldn't be able to play again that season.

"I GUESS PEOPLE LOOKED AT ME IN COLLEGE, AND I COULDN'T SHOOT OR PLAY DEFENSE. I PROVED THEM WRONG."

—JAYSON TATUM

That created more of a need for Tatum, and he delivered. He finished with 14 points and 10 rebounds in that season opener. That made him only the third player in the history of the Celtics, and the first since the great Larry Bird, to have a double-double in his first NBA game. Tatum went on to set the Celtics' rookie records for most three-point baskets and highest three-point shooting percentage in a season.

"Just more was expected," Tatum said.

Then, in just his second playoff series, he faced the 76ers, the team that passed on the opportunity to take him with the No. 1 pick. Tatum ended up averaging 23.6 points in that series, and the Celtics won it in five games. That gave Tatum a chance to send a message to the people who found enough flaws in his game the year before to believe he didn't warrant being the top selection.

"I guess people looked at me in college, said I couldn't shoot or play defense," Tatum said. "I proved them wrong."

He sure did.

As for the Celtics, the risky move turned out to be the right one.

JAYSON TATUM AT-A-GLANCE

BIRTHPLACE: St. Louis
BIRTH DATE: March 3, 1998
POSITION: Small Forward
SIZE: 6'8", 205 pounds
TEAM: Boston Celtics
COLLEGE: Duke
DRAFTED: First round (No. 3 overall) in 2017

CHAPTER 14

KARL-ANTHONY TOWNS

In the NBA, many top players become known by just one name. Sometimes it's their first name. Other times it can be a nickname. When they hear it, fans know right away who the player is.

Shaq. Kobe. LeBron. Magic.

In Minnesota, there is KAT.

Karl-Anthony Towns went to the Timberwolves as the No. 1 pick in the 2015 draft. It didn't take long for him to become one of the best players in franchise history and help end a long playoff absence.

Right from his first season, when Towns was unanimously voted the Rookie of the Year, it was clear he was headed for stardom.

"He's going to be a hall of famer in this league," All-Star Kevin Durant said.

Karl-Anthony Towns brought optimism back to Minnesota fans with his dominant play.

There hadn't been hope like that around the Timberwolves organization for a long time. For years before Towns arrived, the Timberwolves had been not only bad but also unlucky. They had missed the playoffs every year for more than a decade, and they failed to get the breaks that losing teams need to quickly turn around their fortunes.

Heading into the 2015 draft lottery, they had fallen backward eight times previously. They had the best odds to win the top pick this time, but that had meant nothing before. Both times that happened, in 1992 and 2011, they came out of the lottery in a worse position than they went in. On top of that, the team with the worst record hadn't won the lottery since 2004, when the Orlando Magic were able to draft Dwight Howard.

The Timberwolves' bad luck finally turned into good fortune.

The ping-pong balls came up in their favor, and they were able to draft Towns. The big forward had led Kentucky to the Final Four in his only season on campus. He went on to win the Western Conference Rookie of the Month all six months it was awarded and then became only the fifth unanimous Rookie of the Year since 1984.

Towns went right into the starting lineup, and he stayed there game after game, and year after year. He started all 82 games his first three seasons, and when he took the floor on February 7, 2019, at Orlando, it was his 300th straight start. That was the longest streak to open an NBA career since 1970–71, though it ended just a few days later at 303.

A more significant streak, for the Timberwolves, was the one Towns finally helped end the season before. Heading into 2017–18, Minnesota hadn't made the postseason since reaching the Western Conference Finals in 2004. That meant the Wolves had missed the playoffs 13 straight seasons. That was not only the longest slump in the NBA at that time, but the second-longest in league history.

The Wolves' quest to end that drought went down to the final night of the regular season. Minnesota played the Denver Nuggets, with both teams having a 46–35 record. The winner would clinch a playoff spot, and the loser would miss the playoffs entirely and have to wait until next season. The NBA hadn't had a game like that in 21 years.

The game went into overtime before Minnesota pulled out a 112–106 victory. Towns, who was only eight years old the previous time the Wolves were in the playoffs, finished with 26 points and 14 rebounds.

"I'll probably fall asleep tonight and wake up in the middle of the night and start crying," Towns said. "It'll hit me, what happened."

Towns struggled in the first two playoff games, and the Timberwolves lost to the top-seeded Houston Rockets in five games. But that didn't put much of a damper on what had been such a strong season.

Towns was chosen for his first All-Star Game a few months earlier, and on March 28 he set a franchise record for most points in a game by scoring 56 points against the Atlanta Hawks. The Timberwolves rewarded him with a huge new contract in which he could earn about $190 million over five years. He followed that up by making the All-Star Game again in 2019. Before Towns, only Kevin Garnett and Kevin Love had been picked for more than one All-Star Game while playing for the Timberwolves.

> **"I'LL PROBABLY FALL ASLEEP TONIGHT AND WAKE UP IN THE MIDDLE OF THE NIGHT AND START CRYING. IT'LL HIT ME, WHAT HAPPENED."**
>
> **—KARL-ANTHONY TOWNS**

Towns's big 2017–18 season played a huge role in getting the
Timberwolves back into the playoffs.

Towns consistently did the scoring and rebounding expected of a big man, getting 218 double-doubles in his first 300 games. And sometimes he did that scoring in unexpected ways, with much better outside shooting than most players his size. In fact, Towns made 10 consecutive three-pointers at one point during the 2017–18 season, setting another Timberwolves record.

More turmoil surrounded the Timberwolves in 2018–19. Star teammate Jimmy Butler demanded a trade, and the team never found its footing after he

TAKING ON THE WORLD

Towns was an All-State selection and state champion in high school in New Jersey, but most high schoolers never face the level of competition Towns saw during one summer. He played for the Dominican Republic national team in 2012, when his mother's country tried to qualify for the Olympics. At just 16 years old, he played against players such as LeBron James, Kobe Bryant, and Kevin Durant when the Dominicans played an exhibition game against the US team, which won the gold medal. "There are so many things to learn," Towns said, "and I was so happy to be out there and get that experience."

left. Nonetheless, Towns stepped up individually and began taking over games all by himself.

In just a few years, Towns was already one of the best the Timberwolves ever had. They were lucky to get him, but he wasn't going to rely on luck to have the career he wanted.

"Karl doesn't take losing. He's never going to settle," said his father, Karl. "That's the drive in him. That's what drives Karl. He has goals that he's set, and he's not going to be happy until he achieves them."

KARL-ANTHONY TOWNS
AT-A-GLANCE

BIRTHPLACE: Edison, New Jersey

BIRTH DATE: November 15, 1995

POSITION: Forward-Center

SIZE: 7'0", 248 pounds

TEAM: Minnesota Timberwolves

COLLEGE: Kentucky

DRAFTED: First round (No. 1 overall) in 2015

CHAPTER 15

TRAE YOUNG

Trae Young shoots from incredibly long distances. He finds teammates with passes from what seem like impossible angles. Many times, he does both in the same game.

At 6 feet 2 inches tall, the Atlanta Hawks point guard may be small for an NBA player, but he takes big risks and makes bigger plays. Every time he has the ball in his hands, he's likely to make a spectacular play.

"You can say what you want to about size, but when you're the most dangerous person on the court, it doesn't matter," Young said.

That confidence in himself, and the belief he can make any play, carried Young from a historic college season straight through a remarkable rookie year.

Exciting plays are just part of the game when Trae Young is on the court.

A native Texan, Young stayed close to home for college, going to the University of Oklahoma. He averaged 27.4 points and 8.7 assists per game in his lone season with the Sooners, in 2017–18. In the process, he became the first player to lead Division I, the top level of college basketball, in points and assists in the same season. Even his average of 3.9 rebounds per game was pretty good for a point guard.

Not only did Young put up monster stats; he was exciting to watch, too. Young's ability to shoot from far out and make plays with his slick ball handling earned him comparisons to Golden State Warriors

YOUNG BEATS THE BUCKS

One of the highlights of Young's rookie season was his buzzer-beater against the Milwaukee Bucks, who had the NBA's best record during the 2018–19 season. Young grabbed the ball after a pass was deflected and tossed in the winner to give Atlanta a 136–135 overtime victory on March 31. Young finished with only 12 points, and he'd missed all nine shots he had taken since halftime. But he never lost confidence and was hoping for one last chance. He made the most of it. "I know I didn't play well as far as shooting," Young said, "but for me, it's all about the next shot."

superstar Stephen Curry. Sometimes, Young is still a couple of dribbles behind the three-point arc when he pulls up for a jumper.

Still, there were question marks about him when it came time for the NBA Draft. Young is listed at only 6-foot-2 and 180 pounds, so there were concerns that he would most times be the smallest player on the court and could be pushed around. There was also the fact that, after Young's red-hot start with the Sooners, opposing defenses turned up the pressure and were able to slow him down.

Going into the 2018 NBA Draft, words like "polarizing" and "boom or bust" often accompanied descriptions of Young. Experts predicted either he had the electrifying skills to become a superstar or his weaknesses would result in him struggling at the NBA level. The Hawks hoped for the former when they picked him fifth overall.

Early on in his NBA career, the pessimists seemed to be right. Young's three-pointers weren't falling often for the first month or so, and the Hawks were losing often. Making matters worse, Luka Doncic was off to a flying start to his career in Dallas.

The players had been compared since draft night, when the Hawks and Mavericks made a trade. Atlanta selected Doncic with the No. 3 pick but traded his rights to Dallas, which selected Young at No. 5. When Doncic was putting up big stats right away, while Young was still adjusting to the NBA game, people were quick to say that the Mavericks had won the trade and that the Hawks had made a big mistake by passing on their chance to have the better player.

"Obviously, I hear everything that goes on. You can't miss it," Young said in January during an appearance on ESPN's *The Jump.* "Luka's having a really good year so far. And for me, all I do is try to focus on myself and my team. I know it's easy to say, but I'm really dedicated to working extremely hard every day for my teammates and things like that.

"And I think at the end of the day it worked out for both teams," he added. "That's how I look at it. I mean, Luka's doing really well. I feel like I'm doing really well as well."

Pretty soon, Young was doing unbelievably well.

After the All-Star break in February, he was among the top five players in the NBA in assists. With Young leading the offense, the Hawks ranked in the top five

Young started 81 games for Atlanta as a rookie, averaging 19.1 points per game.

in points per game and three-pointers from that point on, despite having a relatively inexperienced roster and a first-year head coach in Lloyd Pierce.

Once Young got rolling, he never slowed down. There were 36-point performances in consecutive games at the end of February, followed by 49 points and 16 assists on March 1 against Chicago. A few days later, he became the first Hawks rookie ever to have a triple-double, with 23 points, 11 assists, and 10 rebounds against Brooklyn.

> **"THE BEST THING ABOUT US IS WE'RE EXCITED ABOUT THE FUTURE, AND I'M JUST HAPPY TO BE A PART OF THIS TEAM."**
>
> **—TRAE YOUNG**

In fact, after his rough start, Young went on to compile some of the top stats that had been seen by a rookie point guard. He scored at least 30 points nine times, the most by an NBA rookie since Blake Griffin did it 14 times in 2010–11. Young finished with averages of 19.1 points and 8.1 assists, joining Oscar Robertson and Damon Stoudamire as the only rookies with those averages. Both of those players won Rookie of the Year Awards.

Young played so well that he even got people who assumed Doncic was the lock for rookie of the year a couple months earlier to wonder if Young had made it a close race. But no matter what, the strong finish for Young and the Hawks had them excited for what was ahead.

"The best thing about us is we're excited about the future, and I'm just happy to be a part of this team. I know a lot of our guys and my teammates are, too," Young said.

TRAE YOUNG AT-A-GLANCE

BIRTHPLACE: Lubbock, Texas
BIRTH DATE: September 19, 1998
POSITION: Point Guard
SIZE: 6'2", 180 pounds
TEAM: Atlanta Hawks
COLLEGE: Oklahoma
DRAFTED: First round (No. 5 overall) by the Dallas Mavericks in 2018

ROOKIE RECORDS

POINTS PER GAME

1. Wilt Chamberlain, Philadelphia Warriors (1959–60): 37.6
2. Walt Bellamy, Chicago Packers (1961–62): 31.6
3. Oscar Robertson, Cincinnati Royals (1960–61): 30.5

MOST REBOUNDS

1. Wilt Chamberlain, Philadelphia Warriors (1959-60): 1,941
2. Walt Bellamy, Chicago Packers (1961-62): 1,500
3. Wes Unseld, Baltimore Bullets (1968-69): 1,491

MOST ASSISTS

1. Mark Jackson, New York Knicks (1987-88): 868
2. Oscar Robertson, Cincinnati Royals (1960-61): 690
3. Tim Hardaway, Golden State Warriors (1989-90): 689

STEALS PER GAME

1. Dudley Bradley, Indiana Pacers (1979-80): 2.57
2. Ron Harper, Cleveland Cavaliers (1986-87): 2.55
3. Mark Jackson, New York Knicks (1987-88): 2.50

BLOCKS PER GAME

1. Manute Bol, Washington Bullets (1985-86): 4.96
2. David Robinson, San Antonio Spurs (1989-90): 3.89
3. Shaquille O'Neal, Orlando Magic (1992-93): 3.53

Accurate through the 2018–19 season

NEW WAVE DREAM TEAM

What might a dream team of players born in 1998 or later look like? Here's what the author says.

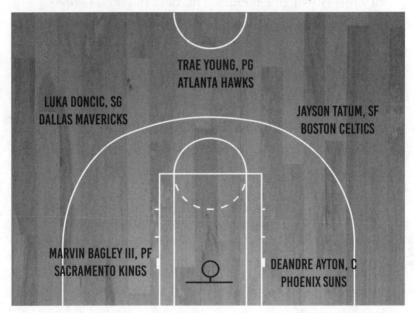

TRAE YOUNG, PG
ATLANTA HAWKS

LUKA DONCIC, SG
DALLAS MAVERICKS

JAYSON TATUM, SF
BOSTON CELTICS

MARVIN BAGLEY III, PF
SACRAMENTO KINGS

DEANDRE AYTON, C
PHOENIX SUNS

RESERVES

G - Shai Gilgeous-Alexander, Los Angeles Clippers

G - Collin Sexton, Cleveland Cavaliers

F - Jaren Jackson Jr., Memphis Grizzlies

F - Kevin Knox, New York Knicks

C - Jarrett Allen, Brooklyn Nets

FOR MORE INFORMATION

BOOKS

Bryant, Howard. *Legends: The Best Players, Games, and Teams in Basketball*. New York: Philomel Books, 2017.

Grange, Michael. *Basketball's Greatest Stars*. Buffalo, NY: Firefly Books, 2018.

Neumann, Thomas. *Basketball Season Ticket: The Ultimate Fan Guide*. Mendota Heights, MN: Press Room Editions, 2018.

ON THE WEB

Basketball Reference
www.basketball-reference.com

Hoops Hype
www.hoopshype.com

Naismith Memorial Basketball Hall of Fame
www.hoophall.com

National Basketball Association
www.nba.com

PLACES TO VISIT

Madison Square Garden
4 Pennsylvania Plaza
New York, NY 10001
www.msg.com/madison-square-garden

The enduring center of the basketball universe, MSG is unsurpassed for its classic game atmosphere during New York Knicks or college games.

Naismith Memorial Basketball Hall of Fame
1000 Hall of Fame Avenue
Springfield, MA 01105
www.hoophall.com

Located in the city where the sport itself was created, the Basketball Hall of Fame is a museum dedicated to the game's history, evolution, and greatest figures. You can even shoot hoops on a variety of baskets through the years, including a peach basket.

SELECT BIBLIOGRAPHY

Beck, Howard. "The Way of the Joker." *Bleacher Report*, 1 Nov. 2017, bleacherreport.com/articles/2741818-the-way-of-the-joker-nikola-jokic.

Cacciola, Scott. "Clint Capela Found His Shot, and He's Taking It." *New York Times*, 7 April 2018, www.nytimes.com/2018/04/07/sports/basketball/clint-capela-rockets.html.

Camerato, Jessica. "Celtics GM Danny Ainge explains trade with Sixers from Boston's perspective." NBC *Sports Philadelphia*, 19 June 2017, www.nbcsports.com/philadelphia/philadelphia-76ers/celtics-gm-danny-ainge-explains-trade-sixers-bostons-perspective.

Krawczynski, Jon. "AP Source: Karl-Anthony Towns is NBA Rookie of the Year." *The Spokesman-Review*, Associated Press, 15 May 2016, www.spokesman.com/stories/2016/may/15/ap-source-karl-anthony-towns-is-nba-rookie-of-the-/.

Mitchell, Donovan. "No Moral W's." *The Players' Tribune*, 29 May 2018, www.theplayerstribune.com/en-us/articles/donovan-mitchell-utah-jazz.

Neuharth-Keusch, AJ. "Dwyane Wade offers high praise for 76ers: 'This is the future of the NBA.'" *USA Today*, 25 April 2018, https://usat.ly/2vK1ORV.

Pelton, Kevin. "Are teams passing on Trae Young missing a future superstar?" ESPN, 17 June 2018, www.espn.com/nba/story/_/id/23813366/2018-nba-draft-trae-young-future-superstar.

Telep, Dave. "Anthony Davis grows into elite player." ESPN, 7 Dec. 2010, www.espn.com/college-sports/recruiting/basketball/mens/news/story?id=5894839.

Young, Royce. "Thunder center Steven Adams is the NBA's immovable object." ESPN, 17 Jan. 2019, www.espn.com/nba/story/_/id/25779289/steven-adams-nba-world-strongest-man.

INDEX

ABOUT THE AUTHOR

Brian Mahoney has been a national NBA writer for the Associated Press since 2005, covering the NBA Finals, All-Star Games, and international basketball events such as the Olympics and world championships. Based in New York, Mahoney covers the Knicks and Nets, along with providing coverage of boxing and tennis events. He is a 1995 graduate of the University of Connecticut, where he started his career covering the women's basketball team that won the national championship.